HOW I MANAGED MY PREVIOUS DATE

Hello all, I just had to write what happened to me on my way to help a friend in need. My girl friend had called and said she needed help moving out, seems her and her husband were splitting up. I had asked my husband to come with me and help and he did not want to come between his friend had his wife. I told him he was being unreasonable and we had a fight the night before and did not enjoy our usual Saturday night date night or the fantastic sex that follows.

I got up early and was in the shower when my husband decided to join me with his hard cock. He scared me when I felt his cock poke my ass in the shower. I thought he was going to go with me to help, so I started to work his cock with my hands and as I was about to give him a wet blow job I asked him if he was going with me and when he said no I handed him a bar of soap and told him to finish himself. Our fight was still on. He told me he was going golfing with a buddy and that I should not be upset with him for siding with his friend. I wore a braless tank top and shorts because it is getting hot in the desert. When my husband saw that I was braless he gave me grief saying I never go braless anywhere with him.

We live in Scottsdale Arizona and my girlfriend lives two hours south in Tucson.
I left Scottsdale around 9:30 and expected to be in Tucson around noon. I had brought a Harlequin book on tape to listen to on my ride. I was about 90 miles south of Phoenix wet between my legs from the sexy voices reading my romance novel over the radio. My 34D breast were at full attention and I would alternate my free hand between playing with my hard clit and tweaking my hard nipples. Just as the girl in the book was about to be violated by her husbands boss I ran over something and got a flat. I pulled over and limped my Avalanche to an off ramp.

I was outside Eloy Arizona in the middle of nowhere. I used my Onstar to call my husband to tell him he needed to come and help me. He was on his third hole which meant his third beer and told me it was a good thing I was braless and that a passing car would stop and help me. I was pissed and hung up on him. He called right back and asked for the exit I was on so he could call

AAA for me. After he called them he called back and told me they would be an hour to an hour and a half. I grabbed a pillow from my back seat and took the bed covers off and was lying in the hot Arizona sun listening to my romance novel as I got a tan and waited for AAA.

I fell asleep and was awoken by two young men who had pulled up behind me in a small RV. The said it looked like I needed help with my tire. I climbed out of the bed of the truck and smiled and told them that AAA was on the way. Then I looked at my watch and noticed it had only been 25 minutes. I must have fallen asleep really quickly. I showed them where the spare was and they went to work I had forgotten to turn the radio down and as they were jacking up my truck the lady in the book was screaming thru an orgasm.

This got the boys attention and when I saw their faces they were blushing. I reached in and turned the radio off, doing so I felt my hard nipples coming back to life. I called my husband and told him that two nice boys had stopped to change my tire and he teased me about showing them my hard nipples and I told them I was old enough to be their mother, he told me I was still very hot and to call when I was back on the road. I watched as they took off the tire from under my truck and was taken by their fine bodies. They both were around 23-25 and very tan, very lean, not real tall but taller than my husband who is 5'8.... They were both wearing shorts and tank tops and flip flop sandals.

I asked them where they were headed and they told me they were minor league baseball players heading to El Paso to report to a new team. After they had gotten the tire from under the truck they asked me for my special lug nut for my custom rims. I did not have a clue what they were talking about and called my husband and he told me it was in the glove compartment I thanked him and hung up. I told the boys it was in there and one of them went to get it. He stuck his head out and said it was not there. He got out and I went to look for it and did not find it I called my hubby and he said to look harder it was there, or wait for AAA and they will be able to fix it. I told the boys this and they told me they would wait and invited me into the RV where it was nice and cool.

I found out their names were Josh and Danny they were 22. I told them my son was 21 and my daughter was 20 both in

college in Tempe. Josh remarked with a mom as good looking as me my daughter must be beautiful. I smiled and said thanks when Danny asked if I wanted a margarita (my weakness)? I said sure since we had to wait. Danny then said we should call AAAA and tell them about my special lug nut so they would be sure they had the right one. He called and said the ETA was now officially 2 hours. Josh poured me a large drink and I noticed it was much stronger than my husband makes, but I had two hours to fill and these young men were so nice to keep me company. I called my girlfriend and told her I would be a few hours late and she offered to come and help. I told her not to bother that I was in good company and she should get as much packed as possible before I get there.

I went back into the RV and the boys were on the bed drinking while I sat at the table with my larger stronger margarita. We talked about each other and I told them I was 46 and have been married for 24 years and had two kids. Josh told me he was from Kansas and Danny was from Texas they were in double A ball which is one step from the big show as they said. They had only met each other 3 days ago when they were notified they were assigned to El Paso. I remarked they seemed like best of friends and made a good team together. Josh said he was a pitcher and Danny was his new catcher and that good chemistry is necessary between pitcher and catcher. As we were drinking there rock music CD ran out and Danny asked me if I wanted to listen to my CD.

 I turned beet red and told him I was ok. Josh asked me if that is what they call a Harlequin book and remarked his mother reads them all the time. I asked how old his mother was and he told me she was 55. I told them that my mother had given me my first book about 5 years ago and that they were and escape from reality. They both smiled. I turned red again and could feel my nipples getting hard again. These two boys had been nothing but kind and helpful and I was becoming aroused in their presence. Danny got up and refilled my drink and Josh said it was time for a shot.

 I declined and they teased me and I relented. Right before I put to my lips to a shot of tequila a DPS car stopped behind us. The boys told me they had been drinking before and I should tell him everything was ok. I walked out of the RV and when the officer approached he asked if we were ok and I showed him my flat and

told him my nephew and his friend were waiting with me. He tipped his dark sun glasses (to my nipples I think) and said he would check back later to make sure I was alright. I went back in the RV and Danny handed me my shot I downed it and knew right away I had too much to drink. I get really horny when I get drunk. My nipples were staying hard now no matter what we talked about. Our talk went back to my book Josh wanted to know what it was about.

I told him about a married lady being seduced by her husbands' boss so her husband would get a raise. Danny asked if there were any stories where a hot milf is seduced by two younger strangers. I was too far drunk and should have known better but I told him it I had not read one like that yet but I think it would be good. Trying to keep it light I asked what a milf was. They both said in unison Mom I like to Fuck... I was red again and my hard nipples now had wetness between my legs to tell me I had taken this too far. Danny then asked if I would show them my tits because my nipples were driving him crazy.

Josh said that for a 46 year old lady I had great tits and that I could wear them braless was testament. I told them I was happily married and then to my own surprise I pulled my tank top over my head and told the boys to do the same. They went one step further and took their shorts and tank tops off. They were down to the very tight gym shorts which held very nice pieces if meat behind them. Josh said he bet I would be wearing Victoria Secret under wear and could they see. I again told them I was a married woman and took my shorts off to prove him right. As I settled back into my seat Danny remarked that my underwear had a wet spot.

I was so embarrassed and was red again. Josh asked if it was them or my book on tape. I smiled and said it was the margaritas that they always make me horny (I did not believe said that). As I said that I noticed the trunks hidden in their Under Armor were growing. Josh asked permission to free his cock and said he would respect my marriage but his cock was throbbing and needed to be released. Danny was not far behind and I was staring at two very hard very nice cocks. My husband is just fine for me I would guess around 7... or so and these boys were thicker and longer by at least an inch with Danny really thick and a little smaller than Josh. Danny asked if he could masturbate on my tits.

I got an idea and put my shirt on and went to my truck and got my book on tape and ran back into the RV as the boys trying to stuff themselves back into their under shorts. They quickly apologized and when I handed Josh the CD smiles came back and shorts came back off. The story was back over the speakers and I went to the back bed and invited the boys to sit on the bed next to me. We listened for a minute or two and I was spell bound as I watched theses two young men slowly work their hands over their cocks. They both were listening to the tape that I had reset to the previous chapter to before I fell asleep.

They were still stroking and staring at my tits and saying that they would love to touch them. I reached over and grabbed each cock and was telling each of them that this was a far as I could go. I could not get hands around either of them they were that thick. I pulled each one to my nipples and started beating their cocks against my nipples which drives me crazy with lust and soon I had an orgasm which I am sure they noticed. Josh warned me he was close to coming and then he erupted a huge amount of cum all over my chest and tummy he bent down and started licking all his cum from my body paying close attention to the nipple that had drove him over the edge.

Danny said he was ready to cum and wanted to shoot off in my mouth. I told him that was not part of the plan and would not be fair to Josh. I then took both of my hands and used some of the wetness from Josh to help him along and he shot off at least as much as Josh if mot more. They both licked my body clean with Danny darting his tongue towards my panty covered pussy a few times. I lie back on the bed and closed my eyes and the tape was at the where the boys found me. The lady on the tape was screaming for her lover to fuck her harder talking like a real slut and begging for more. Josh asked if I liked these stories and I told him that I now had my own story to help me escape. Danny handed me my drink and said another shot was in order.

I quickly downed the drink and chased it with my margarita. I was wet between my legs and feeling very good when I noticed both boys were still pointing straight ahead as hard as they were before they came all over my chest. I commented this fact and Josh said he was good for 3 loads of cum before his cock would not come back right away. Danny said he was good for at least two times maybe more depending on the girl. I told them both

my husband was only good for once a night no matter if I climaxed or not and that sometimes he came in under five minutes leaving me wanting. Both boys said they would fuck me like I have never been fucked before if I would let them.

I reminded them I was almost happily married (even though I was considering the possibilities). I asked the boys how long we have been here when Josh said and hour and 10 minutes, he said he would go and call AAA. While Josh went to my truck to call AAA Danny waved his cock in front of my face and begged me to suck his cock until Josh came back. I told him it would not be fair to Josh and that AAA would be here soon enough. Josh came back and took his shorts off and was hard quickly while telling me that AAA was still over an hour away saying that on Sundays they were shorthanded and they take the closest calls first. I started to get up and get dressed and the boys started protesting.

I told them they needed to get to El Paso and I would be alright. They said no way and I should make myself comfortable and naked so they could jerk off again on my body. What the hell I thought and off came my top and shorts leaving my panties on. I again lay in the middle of the bed while each was on a side on his knees with their cocks at attention and pointing at my tits. Danny asked me to take my panties off and show them my bush as he said he was sure I had a bush. And wanted to see how trim I kept it. I was so hot and horny that I could not believe that these two young cock have been in my presence hard for and hour and I have refrained from doing anything other than touch them, my mind was in control but the alcohol was starting to take over and I knew if they did not leave soon I would be breaking my marriage vows.

I told the boys I would take my panties off and they could jerk off while I played with my clit. I had Danny turn the Cd to the other side and start it again while used my arms to push my boobs together Josh took this as a sign that I wanted his cock between them and he climbed over me and placed his cock between my tits and started fucking my tits slowly and completely pushing his cock almost to my mouth and withdrawing it so when he pushed it back he parted my globes. Danny was watching waiting for his turn stroking his cock I went back and forth between his cock and reaching under Josh and playing with my clit. During one stretch I was close to an orgasm

while playing with my clit I used my tongue to taste the precum from josh's cock.

While all this was happening the girl in the book was screaming thru another climax and I had closed my eyes and was silently mouthing fuck me! Fuck me! Fuck me I thought under my breath but was soon gasping as Danny was stuffing his thick cock into my wet pussy. My mouth started out saying noooo but was soon replaced by a silent powerful climax and chants of yes yes yes yes ooh yes. He was only halfway in me and I had a huge orgasm. Josh reached behind my head and lifted my head so he could feed me his cock and I did not disappoint taking his cock as far as my mouth would allow. Danny was still not all the way in me and I had never felt so full in my life.

My cunt juices were pouring in to accommodate his thickness and soon he was all the way buried up to his hanging balls. He stayed still so my body could adjust to his size and I used the time to enjoy another climax as I was surprised I took his whole cock in me. Josh was still fucking my tits and was spanking my nipples like before and I grabbed his cock and swallowed the whole thing and was using my tongue on his tip and was looking in his eyes telling him silently that I wanted his cum in my mouth. He held my head in place as he emptied his load down my throat. I could not take all of his cum and it started running down my chin and neck. Just as he withdrew his still hard cock (Iwas amazed at his staying power) Danny started fucking my pussy first slowly until I was completely wet then he picked up the pace and gave me the hardest fuck of my life and I was louder than the book on tape girl as he brought my body to orgasm after orgasm.

Josh was waving his hard cock and begging to fuck my ass and I stopped Danny and told them no ass!!! And that if wanted to fuck me he would have to wait til Danny was done. He then High Fived his buddy and took a seat on the bed while Danny fucked me senseless with his tireless cock. I has had at least four orgasms before Danny asked permission to cum in my body. I told him I could not get pregnant and to give me all he has. He then fucked me harder than he had and yelled as he filled my body with hottest load of cum I have ever taken his cum was hot and warmed my insides and brought on another climax.

 Danny withdrew his cock and our combined juices flowed out of my cunt all over the bed. Josh wasted no time in taking his place

and his larger though not as thick cock was a totally different feeling than Danny. While Josh was slowly entering my body I told Danny to call AAA and get an up date. Before he was out of the RV Josh had his cock buried in my body and he was touching me deeper even than Danny just had. Josh was fucking me like he was out for a Sunday drive in the park telling me all along how much he like my body and how he had never had a piece of ass as good as me. I was flattered and really welcomed his understated fucking after the thrashing I got from Danny. Josh was fucking me nice an slow while playing with my sensitive nipples which brought me to my first orgasm with him in me.

He was the perfect lover waiting until my climax had subsided before he picked up the pace and started pounding my cunt harder and harder making me scream out in a sudden climax. Josh again waited for me to finish and started in again at breakneck speed fucking me harder and harder while slapping my tits around I was delirious in ecstasy as he kept this up. Then all of the sudden he slowed way down and was barely at a crawl as he fucked me. I climaxed with the sudden change of pace and was again begging him to fuck me harder.

He pulled all the way out and told me to turn over and get on my hands and knees he wanted to fuck me doggie style (my favorite position with my husband because he can reach my G-spot with his cock). When Josh pushed his cock in me he was resting on my g spot where my husband can reach it by thrusting Josh just had to bury his cock in me and he was sitting right on top of my g spot. He started fucking me and he hit my spot on every stroke and I was in orgasm heaven and could not beg him to fuck me harder because I was speechless from my body being taken over from my continuous climaxes. I had my head buried in a pillow when I looked up and noticed Danny waving his hard cock in my face.

I stared at it for a few of Joshes strokes before I stuck my tongue out and guided it to my dry mouth. I was lost in lust by the fucking Josh was giving me and I tried to take as much as I could of Danny's fat cock. Soon my mouth took over with a mind of its own because my cunt had no intention of stopping the pleasure that it was getting from Josh. My mind separated my body into two parts and I was soon sucking His fat cock as well as I was getting fucked by Josh. I was sucking Danny thru my climaxes from Josh and I was taking more of his thick cock than I ever

thought possible and was soon rewarded with his third load of cum all over my face as he pulled out as he exploded on my face and hanging bouncing tits.

Josh continued to pound into my g spot and keeps my lower body delirious with ecstasy and orgasm after orgasm. I was amazed that my body stayed lubricated during this intense fucking session, with my husband if he has not cum after twenty minutes I start to dry up and its starts to hurt and I have to either have him stop or finish him off in my mouth and my pussy is off limits for at least two days because of the raw skin rash he gives me from his cock. These two bigger and thicker cocks have thoroughly thrashed my body and yet I was still very well lubricated and showed no sign of being raw or even drying out. It probably was the alcohol and the strangeness of it all. Whatever it was I did not want it to end and from the fucking Josh was giving me I was not sure it would ever end.

I was on my way to yet another mind numbing orgasm when josh told me he was about to fill my cunt full of his seed, when he erupted I felt a flood of him cover my whole inner body which brought on another climax as he fell on top of my body and we crashed in to the bed. His sweating body mixed with mine and when his cock popped out of my cunt I felt the flood gates open as his cum came gushing out of my body. I was amazed that his cock was still very hard after having thoroughly trashing my body for at least an hour. He climbed over and fed me his cock to my mouth and I did not waste any time in trying to get another load of cum from his insatiable cock.

Danny who had disappeared was back and had his mouth buried in my vagina bringing my clit towards another climax. I am not sure how I did it but Josh flooded my mouth with another of his sweet loads in less than ten minutes as Danny had my screaming while he nibbled on my clit. Josh and his cock were done and Danny wanted me to suck him again and we ended our tryst with a 69 and both of us coming in under ten minutes. I was exhausted and my 46 year old body needed a hot bath and a warm bed. I watched as the boys stuffed their deflated but still large cock back in there shorts with out their under wear and stood up and found my panties and my tank top and shorts.

Josh came over and put his tongue in mouth and told me I was the best fuck of his life and I smiled and told him if he is half as

good with his women he will never have trouble getting a girl wet. As I walked outside to my Avalanche I noticed the tire was changed, I look at the boys and Danny said while Josh and I were having fun he found the lug nut and changed the tire, I should have noticed his dirty shirt and hand during his last blow job but my mind was focused on his big cock. Danny said my Onstar phone had been ringing but he did not answer it. I told them we needed to call AA A and cancel the call. Josh said it was already cancelled. Then it hit me I was set up and seduced by these two young men. I then told them I did not appreciate their little game and asked them how they knew I would play along with them.

Josh told me that before they woke me up they and watched me for about fifteen minutes and had been masturbating while I was sleeping exposing my neatly trimmed pussy that Danny was so enthralled with. They begged me to forgive them and all I could do was tell them to keep our secret between us and that I appreciated that they stopped for me. As they were getting ready to leave my phone rang I reached in and answered it and it was my husband wondering where I was. I told him I was in a bad area and would call him back soon. I went back to say goodbye to the boys as my phone rang again, it was my friend in Tucson wondering where I was it was now close to 2:30 I got my flat at half past ten. I quickly got the attention of the boys and ask them when they had to be in El Paso, Josh told me they had until 4pm Monday.

I then told them they had to help my friend as they had kept me from helping her. Both boys asked if she was a nice lady like me. I told them they were going to help her pack and move and anything else was none of my business and that they were not to let anything that happened here go anywhere. They assured me our secret was safe. I gave Danny a hug good bye and he thanked me for a memorable time. When Josh gave me a kiss he put his hand under my shirt to fondle my tits. I reached into his shorts and ran my fingers down the length of his hardening cock. I gave them Sharons address and off they went. I got back on the freeway towards Phoenix and called Sharon and told them the boys were on their way, she asked me if she needed to pay them and I assured her I had already taken care of them.

I hung up with her and called my husbands cell he was livid wanting to know where I was and why I did not answer his many phone calls. I told him the key was off while I waited for AAA and

that the boys had found the lug nut and I bought them lunch for changing my tire. After calming hin down I ended our call with telling him I was on my way home and that the he was right the boys liked my tank top. I smiled as I pushed the off button and headed north on I-10. I had barely gone five miles when I was being pulled over by a DPS car. I pulled over and wondered if I was swerving from all the drinking I had done. I sat in my car as he walked slowly towards my truck.. He pointed to an exit about a half mile away and told me to follow him there.

 I had no idea what was going on as I followed him I called my husband and asked him what could happen I did not tell him I had been drinking. He told me to admit nothing and to be as calm and cool as possible. I was a nervous wreck as he walked up to my truck and asked me to step out. He asked me if I had anything to drink and I cannot lie and told him I had a margarita for lunch about an hour ago. He then asked me if I was willing to take a sobriety test. We were standing at his rear door and I was scared and my nipples became hard as I stood on one foot and counted the alphabet. The cop was not paying attention to my test and I thought something was up and stopped and asked him what was going on. He then opened his passenger door and invited me to sit and showed me a pair of binoculars and asked if I always fuck my nephews.

 I was dumbstruck. He then told me when he came on duty the older DPS officer had told him about the Avalanche with the flat and that her nephew was helping her out. He said he drove by the first time not giving us a second look, but when we were still there an hour later he checked with AAA and had been told the call was cancelled he the doubled back and got off the freeway from the north exit and watched to make sure I was alright he said when he saw me fucking my nephew and drinking a shot he knew I lied to the other officer. He said he saw The boy come out and change the tire while the other one fucked me silly as he called it, He then saw as I sucked him after the tire was changed.

 I told him that the boys had fooled me into playing with them and that my husband would kill me if he knew. Then he asked me how did we want to handle this situation. I told him I was fine to drive if he would let me. He told me that watching me handle the two boys had given him a sore cock because he could not take his cock out in his patrol car. I knew where this was going and from my sitting position in his back seat I pulled his zipper

down and freed his hard cock and took it in my waiting mouth and I had my third strange cock of the day. He was also bigger than my husband but not as big as the boys.

I was enjoying this and my panties were becoming wet again. His aroma was different then the boys and I found that stimulating and his uniform made wetter as I swallowed his cock. He really liked my skills and asked if he could fuck me after I suck his cock. I did not pay attention to his blabbering and continued to give his cock my undivided attention and was quickly rewarded with another huge load of cum, not wanting any on my shirt I swallowed his whole load, I licked my lips with my long tongue while I stared into his eyes.

He withdrew his cock and it too was hard as a rock and showed no signs of going soft. He asked if I would fuck him and who was I to say no. I stood up and bent over the back trunk of the car and he asked me to keep my shirt on in case someone drove by. I pulled down my shorts and he tried to put his big cock in from behind but he was too tall and could not bend over enough to get his cock in my 5'7... frame. He had to be at least 6'4... and easily 250lbs but very handsome especially in his uniform. I crawled back into the back seat and got on all fours with my ass up in the air towards the open area. I pulled my shorts down and guided his cock to my clit first and had him fucking my clit for a minute or two until I was on the brink of another orgasm when I used my hand to feed his cock in my vagina and he began fucking me harder and harder.

I was soon out of control as he took over and fed me his cock over and over fucking me into a frenzy of climaxes and orgasms. I had my ass high in the air and he was fucking me downward and I was lost in a state of euphoria as he continued to pound away at my body I was screaming for him to fuck me harder and harder and he had to stop and take off his belt because his baton kept the seat interrupting his rhythm when he put his belt in the floor of the car I noticed his gun and the sight of that shining black metal sent me over the edge and I had my final collapsing orgasm of the day. He had to support my body as he finished fucking my limp body and filling me with another load of cum.

He was sweating profusely thru his uniform and I was a heap in his back seat. After I regained my senses I pulled my shorts up and could feel his cum running down my legs as he thanked me

and wished me well on my way home. I got in my truck and made it home uneventful. I got home at 5pm and had been gone over 7 hours and had the best sex of my life and I was still not sore or the least bit guilty. My husband could have prevented it all had he gone with me or even came to my rescue. My husband asked what took so long and I told him I went to help a friend and ended up making new friends and still helping my friend.

 I took a long hot tub and when my husband came in and started taking off his pants and wanted to join me in my tub as his cock started to grow, as much as I was still horny I did not want to give in to him and I reminded him that I was braless in front of a few men today and they seemed to love my nipples. I slept peacefully that night and the next day Sharon called to say the boys were better than advertised saying they had spent the night and told her that they had thought I was a hot milf but a very nice lady.

 She told me that after they had moved them she cooked them a meal and they went swimming in her new apartment pool and had hit it off with a couple of girls at the pool. She said she came in and was reading (guess what) a book when Danny came back and said that Josh had passed out in a chair by the pool and could he take a shower. Sharon said when the shower stopped Danny came out with towel that did not cover his body and that when she saw his cock she just had to have it. She said he fucked her harder than she had ever been fucked by her soon to be ex. And that his cock was so big she had only seen such a cock in porn's. She said she had to have him before they left and she sent Josh to buy breakfast so she could fuck Danny again. I washed and retired my clothes from that day and keep them close to my Harlequin collection.

Xxxxxxxxxxxxxxxxxxxxxxxxxxxxxxxxxxxxxxxxxxxxxxxxxxxxxxxxxxxxxx

Bob is more committed to his business than his wife. Being lonely she saw Ken playing with his puppy in his front yard. She takes wine and she went to shower. Ken who is not happy married comes in. They continue taking wine while sharing their stories. Become attracted to each other and afterward they goes to bed and starts fucking exercise

I am adjusting the bend, very nearly home. It has been a difficult day at work and I am prepared to return home. My spouse,

Bob, is away on business and my child, Bobby, is away at school. It will be a quiet night time so I can simply lounge around and unwind. As I draw into the carport, I see Ken adjacent playing with his puppy in his front yard. Ken, 20, grew up with Bobby and is a year more seasoned. I have known Ken since he was four years of age. He is into working out and his muscles look hard as a rock. He is wearing a tank best today, of course, to show off his muscles. He likewise has on blurred cut off pants. He is tossing sticks for his canine to get.

I go inside and pour myself an expansive glass of wine. Presently to the washroom, draw a pleasant tub of boiling point water, get in, and unwind while drinking the wine. It feels so great to simply loosen up from the anxiety of the day. As sit in the tub drinking my wine, I arrive at for the cleanser and washcloth and start washing. I wash my face and neck.

At the point when my washcloth secured hand achieves my delicate white breasts, my areolas immediately remained to consideration. Putting the washcloth as an afterthought of the tub, I take an alternate swallow of wine and my exposed hand comes back to back rub my sudsy breasts. I attempt to crush my areola however it is slippery to the point that it continues slipping from between my fingers.

As I softly follow little rings around every areola, I begin to fantasize about making adoration to a fanciful partner. My other hand slips between my legs, between my lips and starts to back rub my clit. I have been fantasizing a great deal of late about making adoration to somebody other than Bob. We have been hitched for 22 years and I was a virgin when we met.

I have never truly made affection to anybody however Bob. The wine must be having an impact on me as of now in light of the fact that I have a climax rapidly.

In the wake of washing, I escape the tub, get dry, and slip into a hot white trim bra and white swimming outfit undies. The doorbell rings. "Who could that be?" I ask myself. I put on my shower robe and go to the entryway. It is Ken.

"Greetings, Ken, go ahead in."

"Hi, Penny. Is this a terrible time?"

"Gee golly. I simply escaped the tub. Tend to a glass of wine?"

"That would be decent."

I pour two glasses. "Come into the family room and take a load off."

Ken sits on the love seat and I sit in the delicate armchair over the room. As I sit in the seat, my robe slides off my legs, presenting them to inside a couple of inches of my underwear. Rapidly coating myself with the robe, I am certain Ken recognized. I know he must have seen my undies. I am humiliated, yet, in some abnormal way, its empowering for Ken to have seen such a private a piece of me. My heart pulsated revives and I trust I am not reddening.

His muscles look hard as steel. He rests his leg on the end table and I can see up one leg of his worn out cut-off pants. He has on no clothing! I can see his balls and the leader of his penis! I think about whether he is doing this deliberately. I attempt to look at him without flinching, however my eyes hold meandering down to his groin. I feel my temperature ascent and I feel flush. I need to battle to keep my eyes in the correct spot.

I get up to get a pack of cigarettes from the end table before Ken. As curve over to get the cigarettes my robe holes open. I know he can see my bra and the swells of my bosoms. I think about whether my areolas are indicating through my flimsy bra. I would like to think not. I am happy I put on my best bra this night. He arrives at for the lighter and offers to provide for me a light. I need to curve down again for him to provide for me a light. As I begin to put my hand on my midsection to keep my robe shut, I choose not to. I recognize his eyes lower to my breasts.

I don't generally mind. I delay a couple of seconds to give him a chance to enjoy the perspective. It provides for me a shiver of fervour to have him gazing at my delicate hills. He truly can see close to he could on the off chance that I had on a swimming outfit. Regardless I consider Ken a young man. He has been one of Bobby's companions for quite some time. His mother is a decent companion and we talk regularly. Our families cook out in the back yard together often.

"I haven't seen you around much of late, Ken, where you been keeping yourself?"

"I have a better half and been investing a ton of time with her."

"Who is she?"

"Goodness, you don't have any acquaintance with her. My guardians dislike her. She is more seasoned than I am."

"The amount more established?" I ask as I take a seat in the armchair.

"She is 36."

"My god! She is simply a couple of years more youthful than I am", I envision.

"I thought perhaps you could help me with an issue I have."

Ken has dependably had the capacity to converse with me about his issues. Actually when he was a young man, he would come to me with issues he felt he couldn't talk about with his mother.

"Without a doubt, what's the issue?" I sneak a look at his groin.

"She gets a kick out of the chance to move moderate and I never figured out how. Would you show me?"

"I'll be happy to. Would you like to begin now?"

"Yea, if it's all the same to you."

      "Alright, I'll put on some decent abate music and show you how to move." I put a CD on and movement him to help me move the end table off the beaten path.
Again my robe falls open when I hang over to get the table and this time I couldn't utilize my hand to keep it shut, in the event that I needed to. Ken again gets a long perspective of my cleavage. I am

feeling somewhat unsure now on the grounds that I may be demonstrating to him excessively.

Primed to give Ken his first move lesson, I remained amidst the floor and he remains before me. I need to take his right hand and put it on my waist. He is extremely strained as I put my left hand on his brawny shoulder and take his other turn in mine. "Simply unwind. You will never be a decent dance expert until you figure out how to unwind." I truly feel odd remaining with my arms around Ken. I hadn't understood how tall he was and shockingly I can tell that his muscles truly are as hard as they look.

After a couple of melodies Ken is doing extraordinary. He adapts quick. We take a seat for a couple of minutes, complete our wine and I pour us every an alternate glass. At this point, I am feeling attracted by him. He unfastens my bra and pushes it aside uncovering the smooth white skin of my uncovered breast to the brilliant room light. He analyzes my breast as his finger softly follows rings around my hardened areola.

It benefits no to battle. I unwind my body. I feel so powerless. How could I have been able to I let myself get into this? Ken grips my bosom for a few minutes. It truly feels marvellous! I am breathing significantly deeper now. I trust he doesn't recognize the extent to which he is turning me on. I need him to stop, yet, I don't need him to stop. It feels so peculiar having somebody so adolescent and nice looking give careful consideration to my exposed breast.

` He delicately presses my delicate hill from distinctive plot and watches it move. He puts his palm over my whole bosom and makes huge moderate clockwise movements, moving it with his hand. He levels it delicately and after that pulls my areola once more. Gracious, it feels SO GOOD, especially when he pulls my areola! I am confounded. I don't know how to stop him and on the off chance that I did, would I wish later that I hadn't?

He is even now touching my completely shown fragile living creature and once in a while squeezing my areola. "When I was ten years of age, I was here playing with Bobby and we discovered some Polaroid's of you."

I know precisely which Polaroid's he is discussing. It was a few nudes that Bob had taken of me. I had constantly trusted that nobody ever saw those photographs! "I have needed to play with your tits

following the time when that day. They are simply a delicate and smooth as I envisioned. Your tits are significantly more wonderful than they were in those pictures 10 years back and your areolas are incredible."

He moves his hand from my breast and simply looks at it. I become flushed. I can't help it. It feels so great to have my bare non-abrasiveness petted by a bulky junior man however I know than I can't permit it and I attempt to battle free one more of a chance. When I battle, he gets a handle on my bosom hard. It harms terrible. I quit battling and unwind my body once more. "If it's not too much trouble Ken, You shouldn't be doing this!" My voice is as of now trembling. "You know you are appreciating this. I can tell by your relaxing."

Am breathing hard, both from battling and from being excited. Ken unties the cinch on my robe and opens it, uncovering my white swimming outfit undies. His left hand leaves my breast and moves down to my waist and afterward significantly lowers. His fingers slide underneath the waistband of my undies."No, Ken, please stop...please don't do this to me...please don't put your hand in my undies. Don't touch me down there!"

I start to tremble all over and my breaths get deeper. My knees are powerless. I have never been under the control of a man along these lines in the recent past. It is both alarming and exciting. I can't escape from his solid grasp. His hand slips into my undies and stops at my flimsy wool pubic hair. He spins his fingers through my hairs and pulls marginally. Not to damage me, yet just playing. His hand investigates my hairy pubic hill and from time to time he pulls a solitary hair. He is taking as much time as required and getting a charge out of toying with me.

"Kindly don't touch me there......it's alright to touch my bosoms on the off chance that you simply won't touch me down there......you can do anything you need with my breasts. ....just PLEASE, PLEASE don't touch me underneath the waist." I trust that on the off chance that I give him a chance to play with my breasts, he will be fulfilled and allow my privates to sit unbothered. I am very nearly shouting.

His finger touches external lips and delicately inspects their shape and surface. He slides down my left lip and returns up the right one.

I attempt to assemble my legs, yet his husky thigh is between my legs and I can't get them together. His fingers gradually investigate my lips. I feel myself getting wet! I am truly getting turned on! This isn't right! I move my hips in diverse bearings attempting to make tracks in an opposite direction from his hand. "Oooohhhh ....", my voice is practically a whisper, "Ken, Please simply play with my breast. Suck on them for me. Kindly suck my tit.

It feels so great when you play with my tit. I adore it when you pull my areola .... Ooooooooohhhhhhhhhhhhhhhhh ...." His fingers drag my wetness verywhere on my shivering lips. "Ken would prefer you not to feel of my breasts? Squeeze my areola." In the same way that I start to challenge one more of an opportunity, his finger slides between my lips, discovers my shivering clit and tenderly back rubs it. The inclination is blissful.

An alternate groan gets away from my lips. "Ooooooohhhhhhhhh............" I am vulnerable. My breathing gets still deeper. He is attacking me freely as his finger gradually meets expectations its path down to my wet vaginal opening. "Uhhhh......" I pant and my entire body tenses for a moment as he effortlessly slides his finger up into me. It is a standout amongst the most wondrous emotions I have ever had.
"You are genuine wet, Penny!" "Oooohhhhhhhhhh .... That .... doesn't mean ..... that I'm .... turned on .... Kindly don't .... It would be ideal if you evacuate .... your finger .... Ken, please .... kindly .... quit doing .... this to me." I attempt to sound like I'm not turned on, yet my voice doles me out.

He gradually slides his finger in and out...in and out....in and out....
Automatically, I spread my legs more extensive and I turn my hips advance and regressive in cadence with his finger. "Ooooooohhhhhhhh ...." My body gets hot all over and wet as sweat spreads me totally. Ken is holding his young physical body against me. He slides in an alternate finger, then an alternate, filling my spellbound opening with his fingers, gradually sliding them finished and done for a few more minutes. He comes back to my swollen clit and I open my legs more extensive and press my pubic bone into his palm. "Ooooooohhhhhhhhhhhh ...."

"I need to kiss it. I need your cockerel in my mouth. Do you get a kick out of the chance to have your dick sucked?" I can't accept I am stating those words. "It's my most loved thing in the entire world."

I bow down before Ken, unfasten his shorts and slide them down to the floor. I am on my knees respecting his excellent huge hard dick, his shaggy balls, and his husky thighs. Taking his monstrous cockerel in my grasp, I move it to my mouth, open my lips and slide them over his swollen purple head and start sucking it like a Popsicle. I relish the dampness on its tip. I enjoy the musk of his pole. Measuring his balls in my grasp, I crush them tenderly as I lick down his long shaft and after that lick every fluffy ball, each one in turn. I take a ball into my mouth and suck it. All the time my hands are kneading his firm butt.

I place his dick in my mouth again and suck as hard as possibleoooohhhhh......you suck so....... well.....I dependably knew..........that you could.......suck a dick!", now Ken is groaning and breathing so hard he can barely talk.
In simply a couple of seconds his dick starts to swell much more and begins twitching. His cum fills my mouth. I overlooked that young people cum much sooner than more seasoned men. I swallow his entire warm salty cum and feel extremely frustrated that he came so rapidly. Snapping over to actuality, I consider what has recently happened. I have done off base.

I have drawn off the young man adjacent. I am ashamed to the point that I let myself escape. Imagine a scenario in which Bob figures out. Will he abandon me? I can't take a gander at Ken. I trust he leaves rapidly. Will Bobby discover? Will I be the subject of neighbourhood tattle? Will Ken tell his companions how he got Bobby's mother to draw him off? Will other young people come over expecting a slippery caress? Imagine a scenario where an entire gathering of young men come over and hold me down. What would they do to me? It's my whole blame for giving him a chance to see the highest points of my breasts prior.

I got him turned on and he couldn't help himself. Ken doesn't take off. He lays me on the floor and stoops adjacent to me. Feeling appallingly remorseful, I close my eyes so I won't need to take a gander at him. He uproots my underwear. He spreads my legs and stoops between them.

I am so mortified there is no option stand up to. I simply lay limp on the floor.

His hands softly skim everywhere on my pussy as he inspects it outwardly shockingly. I have dainty pubic hair and he has some difficulty seeing my pussy in the brilliant sunlight. He spreads open my engorged lips and researches my opening. He twists over and kisses my fleece pubic range. His kisses float between my external lips and down to my wet opening. His tongue gradually dips inside me! It feels incredible. My breathing again is profound. I put my involved his head and run my fingers through his hair.

His tongue meanders all around inside my hot pussy. He slides it taken care of. I feel his tongue work its route up between my wet inward lips, licking rapidly as it gradually creep its path up to my anticipating clit. He licks my clit a few times rapidly with his tongue. "Ooooooooooooooohhhhhhhhhhhh!........that feels........won.......der......ful."He sucks my clit into his mouth and moves it in and out...in and out...in and out....squeezing firmly on it each one time it passes between his wet lips. "Oooooooooohhhhhhhh........don't stop.....please......don't stop!" My hips ascend off the floor to his mouth. I am breathing hard. My skin starts to shiver everywhere. All my muscles strained without a moment's delay. "I'm Cumming! .... Oooooooooohhhhhhhhhhh I'm Cumming! .... I'm Cumming ....suck .... My PUUUUUUUUUUSSYYYYYYYYYYYY!"

After a few minutes of climax, my body unwinds and Ken climbs and lies on top of me. It feels so great to have this solid adolescent body laying on me. I wrap my arms around him and embrace him firmly. My legs are spread and laying level on the floor. We kiss enthusiastically. Ken moves his head down to my breasts. He licks around every delicate areola. At that point delicately sucks an areola into his mouth. He sucks on initial one breast then the other. His tongue flicks every areola. He kisses my neck and sucks on my ear cartilage and I feel his hot breath blowing in my ear. At that point he again kisses me on the mouth. It is a long delicate suggestive kiss.

I wrap my arms around him and stroke his bulky again with both hands. I rub his neck and the over of his head. I feel something move between my legs. He is getting hard once more! Something else I disregarded youngsters. Their hadrons return rapidly. Without

utilizing his hands Ken moves his hips and his penis is rubbing between my still wet pussy lips! We both are breathing enthusiastically once more. "Goodness, Ken ..... put it ...... in me ..... I need .... for you ...... to fuck me ...... It would be ideal if you fuck me." I can just talk between breaths. My legs are spread as wide as I can get them. I arrive at down and take his inflexible dick in my grasp and aide it to my wet opening. He tenderly slides simply the head in. He moves it around true moderate. Never placing it in far.

He is teasing me! He is driving me wild! "Ken.........I want.........it all..........fuuuuckkkkkkkk MEEE!" He penetrates the entire thing inside in one hard stroke. It is superb. It totally fills my pussy. I wrap my legs around his waist and he starts to push. Here and there, good and done. It feels SO GOOD! I can feel the head and veins of his capable dick sliding on my inside dividers. He is extraordinary! Pumping with long influential strokes, he pushes and pushes and pushes. He is driving me wild with energy.

Enduring any longer this time, he measures my breast in one hand and I get his round firm barge in on both my hands. My crotch begins to shiver again and I know I am going to cum an alternate time. My muscles are tensing again and I have that glorious feeling of climax. I feel Ken's dick swell inside me and start its snapping movement that lets me know he is Cumming additionally. Ken falls on top of me with his dick still inside my lazy pussy. He kisses me once more. Does this man-youngster never get tired? I need to assemble my legs yet he is lying between them. His tongue tests within my mouth. In simply a couple of minutes I feel his dick, which is still inside me, swelling one more of an opportunity.

He begins a moderate shallow pumping movement with his hips. "Penny, I have fantasized about fucking you since I looked into fucking. I used to twitch off such a variety of times while pondering you in the wake of advancing here to play with Bobby." "Gracious, Ken, I had no clue!" I had never contemplated me being in another person dream.

He is pumping gradually. One hand is caressing my stripped breast. My pussy is getting wetter and wetter. I can feel his cum from the past time running down the split of my ass and getting the rug wet. His kisses are delicate and long. I stay my tongue into his mouth and rub his again with one hand and the once more of his

neck and head with the other. I am breathing energetically once more!

"Gracious, Ken.......it feels........so gooooood!" I spread my legs wide separated and level on the floor, excessively tired to wrap around his waist. My pelvis is moving in beat with his.

His dick is totally hard again and fills my pussy. My crotch starts to shiver again and I know yet an alternate climax is quick approaching. At that minute he hauls his swollen dick out of my pussy. "Noooooooooooooooo!........please don't stop!"

"Turn over, Penny, and lay on your stomach." I do as trained. Ken is in complete control of me as he has been the entire time. I feel the delicate hide of the rug against my swollen tits. It feels warm. I spread my legs as wide as could be allowed to acknowledge his enormous dick into my willing cunt. He stoops between my legs then lies on top of me. I feel his dick between my pussy lips. He is slides it between my lips then into my delicate pussy.

I am laying level on the rug on my stomach with my legs spread as wide as could reasonably be expected. He gradually moves his full-become dick done and finished, here and there. I move my butt all over in beat with him. It feels solo great. My skin begins to shiver. I need to embrace him yet I am on my stomach and can't achieve him. I am close climax once more. He hauls out before I cum.

"Nooooo....don't stop!......i want........to cum!" He turns me over and puts his knees on each one side of my head.

His gigantic dick is directly before my mouth. I hold it in my grasp and lick my adoration squeezes off his pole. He twists over and presses his tongue between my swollen pussy lips and starts licking my clit. I open my mouth and acknowledge his dick into it as he does the same with my cit. am doing 69 with the child adjacent! He moves his hips all over. He is fucking my face! I cherish it! I feel my groin shivering once more. My muscles tighten, I detached my breath. I am going to cum. I feel his dick swell in my mouth. I begin an alternate climax.

Ken keeps on licking my pussy and suck my clit into his mouth. His gigantic dick begins yanking and his cum strikes the once more of my throat. I swallow each drop. I am as of now Cumming! Ken's dick starts to psychologist and he falls with his full weight on me and his delicate dick the distance in my mouth. His

pubic hair is tickling my button and his balls on my nose. I am even now Cumming! Ken is even now sucking my clit. I have never cummed this long previously. I have never cummed this commonly previously. I am even now Cumming! I can't relax. My heart in beating. I am as of now Cumming! Ken's delicate dick is still in my mouth.

I am even now Cumming! I suck firmly on his dick. My legs are starting to spasm from being so strained so long. I put my arms around Ken and embrace him as tight as possible. I keep sucking his limp dick. At long last the waves of climax are abating. I thought I would pass on! It was the strongest climax I have ever had in my life. My body at last unwinds. Ken's dick is still in my mouth. I suck simply a couple of more minutes and he shoots a little load in my mouth and he unwinds with his head at my pussy and his dick still in my mouth.

Ken, so gently, follow my sore pussy lips with his finger. I know he is inspecting it and I am cheerful that he needs to. I need him to know each fold of skin in my most private zone. I expel his dick from my mouth an analyze it. I look at his textured balls and study where they meet his butt. I feel the nuts in his sacks. I investigate the veins in his bulge. After something like 30 minutes of both of us investigating and contemplating one another, Ken gets up, gets dressed, strolls over and provides for me a sweet kiss on the mouth. I am even now lying bare on the lounge floor. "Much appreciated Penny, you're really great. I need to go home now. Mother will be pondering where I am." "Much obliged to you, Ken. You were eminent. I must have a tame streak in me.

I adored being under your control like that. I trust we keep this little scene simply between us. In the event that any other individual figured out, it could result in a ton of issues." "Great. You were incredible. Don't stress, it'll be our mystery. Bye now and let us meet again for pleasure."

XXXXXXXXXXXXXXXXXXXXXXXXXXXXXXXXXXXXXXXXXXXXXXXXX
XX

I had the most phenomenal sex of my life and I need to tell somebody. My name Kelly, 43 years of age and have what my spouse of 24 years call is a slayer body. I attempt to keep myself in incredible condition. I am pleased with my 34dd 23 35 figure. We have an extremely decent sexual coexistence because of my spouse's creative energy.

He generally needs me to do something else. I am normally excessively of a ruined game in all actuality, however in my dream I adore all that he recommends. We have four children the most youthful of which is a 19 year old school sophomore. He exists on grounds about 10 miles away. Our house is really enormous with a considerable measure of area and an exceptionally pleasant back yard for gatherings.

On the Saturday before Halloween our children asked if they could host the house for a gathering. My spouse and I host constantly revelled in the outfit gatherings and promptly gave our consent. We got hitched when I was just 18 and had our children extremely junior. The children all welcomed their companions and we were advised to expect simply fewer than 100 individuals.

We enlisted a food provider to grill nourishment and a D J to keep the music set and a barkeep to check I D's on my child's companions. My three little girls were all wearing outfits from T V shows; my child was wearing a football pullover and a head protector. My spouse was a specialist. I was a madam from the Wild West. I wore a long streaming dress that finished at my breasts which were in pushed up simply right. As we were getting dressed my spouse said I was certain to make a couple of our children companions gaze at my cleavage.

I let him know he was insane, that I couldn't compare to the youngsters impending. He wager me our standard wager that I have the consideration of youthful men throughout the night. He called me a milf under his breath. I requested to talk up and he let me know to be glad for it. I had no clue what he was discussing.

The children began touching base around 7 and before 9 the back yard was jumping. The children in the basic ensembles were playing ball and volleyball, while the more expound outfits us sticking around the move floor and the bar. My spouse and I concurred he would stay in the house to ensure his bar from the swarm. I was the entertainer and was having an extraordinary time.

The barkeep continued making my margarita's stronger and soon I was felling tanked. When I have an excessive amount to drink I get exceptionally horny and coquettish. With all the exact youthful fellows at the gathering my loins were getting prepared and I was wet simply taking a gander at the volleyball court and all the gentlemen without shirts.

My spouse is 44 and looks great, however these young men have no fat at all and their bodies are tore. I required to discover my spouse to have him fulfil this urge. I discovered him viewing a football diversion in his bar. He knew after I was in his vicinity just 10 seconds that I was primed to rip his jeans off and fuck him. He began teasing me about the entire youthful rooster out back making me horny. I let him know they were our child's companions, and he ought to observe the rules.

He got my hand and headed me to the room and lifted up my dress and covered his face in my sopping wet cunt he ambushed my container and I was soon attempting to turn him around so I could get a grip of his extremely decent 7" chicken. I got his rooster in my mouth almost as he was bringing me to my first climax.

I gulped down his entire cockerel and he attempted to push it deeper down my throat. I utilized my hand to crush his balls and he went crazy when I grasp his balls. He attempted to push his cockerel deeper and let my tongue have an attempt with his rooster. I suck him for an additional 10 minutes without agreeing with me. I discharged his cockerel from my mouth and he stood up and lifted up my dress so he could direct his rooster in my wet cunt. He brought me to the verge of an alternate climax simply by putting his cockerel in my needing cunt.

Jeff cherishes my tits and as he fucked me he attempted to untie my bodice to free my hurting tits from my dress. While we are going solid we heard children go into the house and discover his completely loaded bar. I advised Jeff that we had an unpredictable look out for them. He would have none of that as he is truly fucked me harder and without stopping. I closed my eyes and focused on the fucking my spouse was providing for me and methodology my third climax as Jeff let me know he could keep going any longer and he backed way off and tweaks my areolas as this sends me to my peak.

At that point he grabbed his beating and soon I filled his hot cum filling my body. He felled on top of me and we both simply laid

there for a couple of minutes before he got up to go and secure the bar. I got up and went to the washroom to clean up and set my girdle back on. In the restroom I knew I was still exceptionally horny and needed to tease my spouse so I took off my undies and left my undergarment a little looser on top.

I needed his rooster in my cunt of whatever I left of the night. When I joined the gathering, a gathering of fellows had begun a poker amusement at the lounge area table. Our child is an enormous card player and he was behind the diversion. My spouse chose to play likewise among the gathering of 9 players. I kissed him pressed his groin and longed him good fortune.

I meandered once more outside searching for our young ladies and discovered they had left to go to an alternate gathering that they had Rasp's to prior. They let me know they would be back in something like 90 minutes. With an alternate margarita under control I studied the entire gathering and was welcomed by all the children with what an incredible gathering and back yard we had.

I was feeling glad and extremely upbeat as I conversed with all the children. I was remaining behind our huge palm tree when I heard a gathering of young men discussing the gathering. They were enjoying a reprieve from the volleyball. It took all I needed to not gaze at the hard sweating midsections then my jaw dropped as I heard that saying once more.

One of the young men said Danny's mother is a genuine milf and he was soon high filing the other three gentlemen he was talking as well. I was supposing what is a milf? I gobbled my beverage and got up enough fearlessness to ask them. I stepped aroused.

I snatched an alternate beverage from the barkeep and was viewing the moving when Mike requested me to move. I wanted to move and when my spouse saw me moving he was on a break from his diversion and went to the DJ and provided for him an arrangement of my main tunes. He came up to me while I was hitting the dance floor with Mike and let me know to have a great time and continue moving until he beat all these children at poker then he was going to fuck my brains out like these adolescent studs need to.

I grinned and did a reversal to my move accomplice. The following tune was my top pick "My Sharona" from the 70's. It's a quick tune everyone knows and I wanted to move to it. I was teased on the floor and with Mike I was no diverse. We had an

extraordinary time when the following melody my spouse asked for went ahead. "Discussion" by Prince. An alternate fave when I'm horny. With my spouse on the floor with me I turn into this tune. With Mike I attempted to keep it clean however it was hard.

Towards the end of the melody, Mike whispered in my ear "mother I'd get a kick out of the chance to fuck". I didn't recognize what he was discussing yet my body was all of a sudden throbbing. My shocked look made him say the expression Milf and "mother I'd jump at the chance to fuck" then it hit me. I had a climax hitting the dance floor with this adolescent man.

I continued rehashing the truism "mother I'd get a kick out of the chance to fuck" again and again to myself. A moderate tune went ahead and liked a courteous fellow Mike requested this move and soon his mouth was on my detached fitting undergarment as he was attempting to cover his face in my midsection. I was in a state of mass perplexity I was cherishing the consideration he was providing for me but then I was doing things I just had done with my spouse. I am groping his hardness press against my body throughout the move.

He again whispered those words to me "mother I'd get a kick out of the chance to fuck". He was hitting each nerve in my body. I was moving not 25 feet from my spouse and child with a 21 year old stud who was disagreeing with me. I needed to fuck him. I chose to take Mike to our visitor house and fuck him and demonstrate to him I could be a true live milf.

I advised Mike to reach me in five minutes in the visitor house through the carport. He was grinning as he went away. I back-pedalled to scout my spouse. I let him know I cherished him a whole lot and was having an extraordinary time. He let me know to go back to teasing all the young men outside and to be primed for him later. I guaranteed him I would.

I did a reversal outside to the barkeep for an alternate solid toast provide for me more boldness to do this. My body was throbbing for this, yet my brain was not certain. When I strolled into the room I was stunned to see Mike as well as Jay and John too. Turns out Mike advised the fellows he was going to rest in the visitor house and they concluded that they were tired likewise.

I simply grinned when John let me know again what a milf was. He said I was prime milf material. He then requested to

demonstrate to him my tits. I let him know I would be happy to demonstrate to him my tit on the off chance that he demonstrated to me his rooster. He squandered no time in discharging his rooster from his shorts. I was awestruck at his size he wasn't excessively substantial yet thick and gave off an impression of being hard.

He strolled over to me and inquired as to whether he could touch my tits and when I arrived at for his chicken he had his reply. Mike and Jay were understanding left when I motioned for them to go along with us. I was playing with Jon's thick quickly extending rooster brought my tongue to my mouth as I was going to enjoy this thick bit of steel. I had now felt Mike's hard rooster on the move floor. He was about the same size as Jeff however ooh so hard. Jay had a greater chicken than both of them I was currently going to have sufficient energy of my life.

I guided the young men to the quaint little inn directions to every one of them. They were just ready to tune in. I had Jon and his thick rooster at the foot of the bunk as I needed to suck him first and fuck him keep going so he would not extend me for the other two. I needed to fuck Mike first and had him lie in the bunk with his young rooster indicating straight up. I advised Jay to be patient as I would get to him soon. As I mounted Mike's cockerel it felt so great that I needed to simply sit on it and have climax after climax.

I inclined forward and tried for Jon and his thick chicken. He was hard as steel and I cherished the extent of him he was so thick however he fit in my mouth so great. He was in paradise as I was skipping on Mike'scock as I was sucking him. He squandered no time in snatching my tits as I continued sucking him. Mike was playing with my clit as I ricocheted on his cockerel and he brought my first peak not long after his finger discovered my sweet spot.

Perfectly fine peaked Jon filled my mouth to flooding with an immense heap of his sweet tasting cum. Jay squandered Jon time in putting his cockerel where Jon had been. His cockerel was the greatest and felt great going down my throat as I could feel him hit spots that were virgin to cocks in my mouth. He was slapping my swinging tits as Mike had gotten the pace of my fucking and I had an alternate peak when he ejected in my cunt.

Jay needed to fuck me at this time and I got on my knees and let him know to fuck me from behind. When he mounted me, his cockerel was so profound within my body that I had a gigantic

climax as he arrived at the back divider of my vagina. While he was fucking me and bringing me to peak after peak, Jon was hard again it had just been 5 minutes. This was phenomenal as I return his rooster in my mouth and I held his balls as I sucked him to the beat of my cunt getting beat by jay.

Jay then arrived at under and snatched my thrashing tits and hung on while he shot his heap in my effectively splashed cunt. Jon needed to fuck me and I had him rests and brought down my self on his thick chicken. It was tight and took some tender pushing to cover his chicken in my body. He has extended my rooster that I recognized what I needed next. I ricocheted on his thick chicken for something like 20 minutes when I put my tit in my mouth and licked my areola with my long tongue it was excessively for him and he shot an alternate tremendous heap of cum in me.

When I pulled off him I told Mike and jay they were searching for me then went to bunk. I went to the restroom and ran the shower and cleaned up before I got into couch. My spouse returned to life and planted his face on my cunt and presented to me a huge peak. I cleaned my self so that the young men cum was all gone. At the point when my spouse mounted me he was certain to say that I made a considerable measure of adolescent men joyful today evening time with my outfit. On the off chance that he recognized my detached cunt he doesn't say anything and soon included yet an alternate heap of cum to my body today. It began with a heap from my spouse and finished the same way. At the same time in the middle of I realized what a gentle is.

Incidentally I would get an impression of her pants, she didn't know yet on more than one occasion a year was an incredible help to my winking dreams. I am a bit of a knickers fixated man, from numerous points of view I want to see pants than pussy - particularly when they are white. I sat inverse Kelly, as you do, to position myself at the right plot for a sight, however, she kept her legs stuck together whilst she consumed, the sun was hot, and almost as I was surrendering it happened...

She folded her legs... gradually... furthermore there it was, an incredible take a gander at her pants, and what a superb sight I got, white, vigorously bound, the kind of sight I think most men would see as their 'perfect situation', indeed the pants were so well in sight. I was practically humiliated so I turned away after several seconds

so nobody perceived what I was taking a gander at. My rooster was wet and beginning to solidify. At that point the vision ceased as she put her leg down once more. Despite the fact that they weren't on perspective I began to retain what I had seen. The ideal shot, enormous white triangle, pants vanishing between her legs and a full 'grounds', as such on the off chance that she wasn't wearing her knocks I would see her entire pussy.

At that point a few minutes tater she folded her legs once more, this time I was bolder and got around a 5 second glimmer, with time to retain the sight, this time. I saw the dull shadow of her pussy indicating through her pants. At that point at long last, she put one foot onto the seat of her seat to pick her toes. What's more this time I got an alternate blaze of the flimsy band between her legs all smashed up where it secured her split. If I could have touched my chicken, I would have cum in seconds.

That was it then, the best up skirt a man could wish for. I didn't get a chance to wink for a couple of hours, yet god it was great when I did! I was upbeat to have another memory for my dream - and accept it or not, it showed signs of improvement...

One day from now, Sunday, Kelly rang to attempt and gets me to settle her machine via telephone, not that extraordinary. At any rate I required to go adjust there to evaluate it and attempt to sort it. Kelly made me a beverage and all was well, hubby then needed to go to deal with the evening movement.

I was truly humiliated at being discovered. I conceded that I had seen her pants and apologized - I said I couldn't stop myself looking, I was sad yet most men would look wouldn't they. I said I was sad that I had affronted her.
She said, she wasn't insulted, she said she perceived me looking and simply to look at me she deliberately put her foot on the seat to check whether I looked. I said sorry once more, indeed I had seen them 3 times that day.

At that point she said "would I be able to ask an alternate inquiry"?
"Yes" I said anxiously...
"Where they like these"?
what's more with that she roosted on the arm of the couch, loaned back a bit to give her a chance to skirt ascent and afterward she

opened her legs something like 6 inches to uncover her pants, white once more, yet hard for me to check whether they were the same.

My heart was beating, what do I say? It is safe to say that she is going onto me? On the off chance that I pull out all the stops and she isn't she would tell my wife and I would be profound into a bad situation.

Thus, rather reluctantly I said...

"Yes, I suspect as much"

"Don't you know"? She said, "Either they are or they are not" she said.

"I can't see them exceptionally well" I said. My juices where climbing I was getting wet, god, I recollect trusting she could see any wet fix in my trousers.

She shut her legs and remained up with that she came closer to me and proposed I may require a more critical gaze to look at them. Kelly simply remained there and inquired as to whether in any case we had a sexual coexistence. I said very little, Kelly said, "Murmur, she doesn't much like sex does she" I said "not with me at any rate" attempting to be interesting to blanket my uneasiness.

At that point she lifted up her skirt, gradually, however the distance and there she was before me, pants on full show, legs marginally separated. Fuck me, I thought, am I imagining?

"Well", she said, "would they say they are the same"?

Yes I conceded, they are, not having any desire to move.

"Have a long look", she said, "however don't touch me" she said

I devoured my eyes on the exquisiteness of her legs, her pants, her cunt lump and the slight space where her break lay underneath.

After what appeared as though ages, she moved. She moved on the back of me and sat on my lap. My rooster was widespread, my heart dashing, my brain in overdrive.

"Look, I may not bonk Clare much, yet I do love her and would not have any desire to damage her" I said.

She made me take a gander at her eyes and gradually said "I would prefer not to damage her either. I don't love you, I would prefer not to wed you, I simply ridiculously need to fuck you", she said

"I can feel your rooster against my pants - don't let me know you would prefer not to fuck me too"?

I simply nodded

I didn't require any more clues; I went to get my hand in her pants. "No", she said, "Time for that later" and with than she dropped to the floor and proceeded onward my lump. She pulled down my zip and backed off solid rooster out of my wet boxers. I'll never forget the following minute when her lips touched my handle as her hand held the pole pulling my foreskin down so her tongue could investigate me.

She played with my cockerel with her teeth, tongue and lips, and it wasn't numerous seconds before I felt the certain occurrence.

"I'm going to cum" I said, providing for her the alternative to withdraw. Gratefully she kept up the BJ and I pushed her head down as I began to cum in her mouth. My cum didn't trouble her whatsoever, she continued sucking and licking all the time that I was jolting my sperm into her mouth. She was the feline who had got my cream!

After I had gone delicate in her mouth she found and said "perhaps you won't be so timid now" - I wasn't! I rapidly got stripped whilst in the meantime letting her know to stay dressed - "I manage your garments soon" I made a guarantee to her. I didn't need my garments to act as a burden when my rooster got prepared to fuck her.

''What are you going to do with that" she said taking a gander at my limp chicken. "Take after me" I said heading her into the parlour.

I laid her on the couch and went down on my knees adjoining her. I pulled up her slipover to get my eyes on her bra. Tenderly I moved onto her tits and began playing with the little ones she had, exchanging between my fingers and my mouth, sucking them for a couple of seconds through her bra.

She groaned delicately and sexily. "Time for you to appreciate my mouth now" I said as I fixed her bra and discharged her firm areolas from their holders.

I took a shot at her tits for a moment or two, yearning to get down to her pants and pussy, yet not having any desire to be so essential so soon.

She was getting more stimulated and gentling moving her leg all over a bit. As I kept playing on her tits, I gradually moved my hand down her skirt and down her leg, delicately touching her legs all

around yet being mindful so as not to touch her pants - I needed her as hot and randy as could be expected under the circumstances before I concentrated on that bit!

I could smell she was getting wet between her legs, that heavenly possess an aroma similar to wet lady provided for me my sign to gradually move my head far from her tits and down to her cunt.

Presently was the time to move my touching delivers between her legs, I ever so tenderly touched her pants directly between her legs, and shockingly felt her wetness. She was extremely wet, her pants were splashing wet and I felt ruler of the cocks!

"Fuck you're wet" I said as I lifted up her skirt and devoured my eyes again on those incredible white fancy pants. Gradually I manoeuvred one hand into the top on her pants, as I touched her pubes shockingly I couldn't accept that I was so fortunate to be in her pants. I stroked her pussy and pushed a finger down into her split. I passed by her clit and wrinkled through her folds and discovered her cunt opening.

"Appreciate" I said as I pushed my finger good and done with her wet cunt.

After a couple of seconds I hauled my hand out of her pants - she wheezed in joy as I put one finger inside each one side of her pants and tenderly pulled them down a couple of inches. At last I got full on take a gander at her pussy, a dull blonde bramble, getting darker as it secured her folds and went between her legs.

"What a phenomenal pussy" I said. She said "please make me cum - or my head is going to blast" I pulled her pants down and dropped her splashing pants onto the floor. I put one arm around each one leg and pushed my head between her legs and up towards her cunt.

Tenderly I began to move my tongue into her pussy, kissing everything over, getting her wetness everywhere all over all the while. At last I pulled her folds separated. Climax in the way that makes any man feel as though they have truly done well. "Fuck me you're great" she said, "Fuck I'm fortunate" I said, thinking back up at her cunt.

My rooster had got hard again throughout the oral sex I provided for her. "Presently for the genuine article" I said as I got up and manoeuvred myself on top of her body, she in a split second

opened her legs wide letting my legs and rooster drop into position. "It's years since I've needed a rooster inside me to the extent that I need yours now" she said "fuck my cunt and fuck it well" she said.

I was as hard as I've ever been as she drew her knees up and open her legs more extensive. I lifted my body up a bit and guided my rooster to her clit and after that slid it down to the doorway of her opening. She began gasping and wheezing again - simply a couple of minutes after she had cum some time recently.

Tenderly I pushed my rooster and I felt her cunt open to permit my cockerel to slide into her. She was still exceptionally wet so there was almost no safety.

I slid my cockerel into her cunt gradually, as this dependably makes a rooster feel any longer than it truly is - when you've just got 6 inches you need to capitalize on every last bit!

I pushed it in the extent that it would bet everything one trust, until our pubes met. Surprisingly I kissed her tenderly on the lips and said "I trust you delight in this to the extent that I am going to". "I as of now am" she wheezed. She bolted her stunning legs around my lowest part and pushed hard to get my cockerel into her cunt the extent that this would be possible.

We then began to fuck one another, I pushed my chicken good and done gradually to begin and she reacted by moving in beat. On more than one occasion my cockerel slipped out and I made a purpose of pushing it into her clit each one time whilst attempting to discover her cunt opening once more. It was just a few minutes before I felt my climax nearing. She recognized and said "Please come inside me". I began to build my rate as I kept on fucking her phenomenal cunt. I at long last began to cum inside her as she kept on moing my rooster lock stock and done with her, she was panting louder and louder as I came inside her.

In the same way that I began to subside she let out an enormous pant as she embraced me and came too. At the end of the day her beats of climax experienced her few times before we both fallen into every others arms. We embraced for a moment or somewhere in the vicinity before discharging one another.

As I last signal I pulled her pants again on to keep my sperm inside her as she sat up and cleaned herself up whilst I got dressed. We consented to keep this session as one-off as we both needed to much to detached my having an unsanctioned romance and danger

being discovered. The memory of my chicken sliding into her cunt surprisingly will stay with me work the day I pass on......We shared stories for a moment and one went like this;

A businessman met a beautiful girl and agreed to spend the night with her for $500. They did their thing and before he left, he told her that he did not have any cash with him, but he would have his secretary write a cheque and mail it to her, calling the payment "RENT FOR APARTMENT "

On the way to the office in the morning, he regretted what he had done, realizing that the whole event had not been worth the price. So he had his secretary send a cheque for $250 and enclose the following typed note:
"Dear Madam, This is a cheque for $250 for the rent of your apartment. I am not sending the amount greed upon, because when I rented the place, I was under the impression that:
1. It had never been occupied.
2. There was plenty of heat; and
3. It was small enough to make me feel cosy and at home.
However, I found out that;
1. It had been previously occupied.
2. That there wasn't any heat, and
3. It was entirely too large.

Upon receipt of the note, the girl immediately returned the cheque for $250 with the following note:
"Dear Sir; First, I cannot understand how you could expect a beautiful apartment to remain unoccupied indefinitely.As for the heat, there is plenty of it, if you know how to turn it on.Regarding the space, the apartment is indeed of regular size, but if you don't have enough furniture to fill it, please do not blame the management.Please send the rent in full or we will be forced to contact your present Landlady.

www.ingramcontent.com/pod-product-compliance
Lightning Source LLC
Chambersburg PA
CBHW050858290526
45792CB00002B/650